# A BOOK of DOGS

# (AND OTHER CANINES)

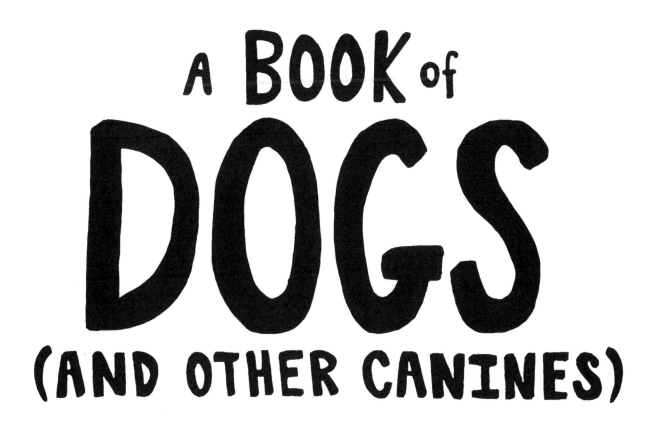

Katie Viggers

Laurence King

For Mum and the best dogs ever: Bob, Duke, Toby, and Meg xx

LAURENCE KING

LAURENCE KING
First published in the United States in 2023 by Laurence King

HB ISBN 978-1-510-23038-5
E-book ISBN 978-1-510-23081-1

10 9 8 7 6 5 4 3 2 1

Printed in China

Laurence King
An imprint of
Hachette Children's Group
Part of Hodder and Stoughton
Carmelite House
50 Victoria Embankment
London EC4Y 0DZ

An Hachette UK Company
www.hachette.co.uk
www.hachettechildrens.co.uk
www.laurenceking.com

# Contents

# Meet the canines

There are over 30 species of canine. The one we know best is the pet dog, but this family of animals also includes some wilder relatives, such as wolves, foxes, coyotes, dingoes, and jackals.

Wild or domesticated, this furry family is fascinating. So, let's meet the canines!

Us canines don't all live in the same place. We just got together to help make this book.

Staffordshire bull terrier

Gray wolf

Red fox

Pug

Afghan hound

Border collie     Chihuahua     Great Dane     Poodle     African painted dog

# Working dogs

Working dogs are a group of strong, intelligent canines originally bred to help humans with physical tasks.

Some of these hardworking dogs were first bred in colder climates. They can now be found around the world and are often kept as pets.

Newfoundlands are very big dogs. A male can weigh up to 150 lbs—that's as much as an adult human! But they are laid back and friendly and can make good pets.

## SIBERIAN HUSKY

Siberian huskies have very thick fur that keeps them warm in the extreme cold of the Siberian Arctic. They were bred to pull sleds and can run for hours.

## NEWFOUNDLAND

These handsome dogs come from Canada. They are very strong and helped fishers pull in heavy nets full of fish. Great swimmers, they even have webbed paws!

## SAINT BERNARD

These gentle giants originated in Switzerland. Saint Bernards were first kept as pets and guard dogs by monks living high up in the snowy Alps, before becoming rescue dogs.

## EYE COLOR

Siberian huskies have the most beautiful eyes. They can have brown eyes, blue eyes, one of each, or even parti-colored eyes— that's two different colors in the same eye!

Lapland

Great St. Bernard Pass

Saint Bernards make great mountain rescue dogs. Their amazing sense of smell helps them find people trapped in snow drifts. They also have enormous paws to dig them out with.

Even working dogs need a day off to play!

Huskies were used to pull sleds in Siberia, Greenland, and Alaska. In some remote areas, these energetic pups are still used as a way of getting around today.

# Herding dogs

Herding dogs were originally bred to work on farms and ranches.

This group of dogs are also popular pets. Be warned—they need lots of exercise and have a strong instinct to herd!

I like to keep busy, and I can help with the laundry.

## BORDER COLLIE
The highly intelligent border collie is a British herding dog. It is mostly black and white with a white tip at the end of its tail.

## AUSTRALIAN SHEPHERD
Despite its name, the Australian shepherd dog actually came from Spain and the USA.

Herding dogs, such as border collies, need a lot of physical and mental stimulation. They are obedient and easy to train.

## BEARDED COLLIE
Originating from Scotland like most collies, the bearded collie gets its name from the shaggy fur around its face.

## ROUGH COLLIE
Rough collies originated in the Scottish Highlands as a traditional sheepdog. They became very popular pets in the US after the TV show *Lassie* had a rough collie as its star!

## ROYAL FAVORITE
Queen Elizabeth II famously loved corgis. When she was 18 years old, she was given her very own corgi, which she named Susan. After Susan, the Queen had over 30 corgis in her lifetime.

The border collie has such a strong instinct to herd that it will mistake household objects for things that need to be rounded up!

Collies are at their happiest when herding animals. They work well together as a team to round up and protect livestock such as sheep and ducks.

# Hound dogs

A hound is a type of hunting dog. They come in all shapes and sizes.

There are two main types of hound—the scent hound, which has an excellent sense of smell, and the sight hound, which can track prey by sight. Today these dogs are mostly kept as family pets.

## DACHSHUND

With its long slender body and short sturdy legs, the dachshund is often called a sausage dog. They are scent hounds, once used to sniff out small animals from their burrows.

## BEAGLE

These scent hounds are friendly, cheerful dogs who love the company of their owners. Snoopy, a character from the popular comic strip *Peanuts*, was a beagle.

## GREYHOUND

Greyhounds are the fastest of all the canines—they can run up to 45 miles per hour! These speedy sight hounds can also see very well in the dark.

Scent hounds

The bloodhound is the largest scent hound. It has long jowls and drools a lot!

Could somebody please pass me a handkerchief?

At around 8 inches tall, the dachshund is the smallest scent hound.

A basset hound's floppy ears help sweep smells from the ground up to its sensitive nose.

## SENSITIVE NOSE

Beagles make the best sniffer dogs. It is believed that, when trained, they can identify up to 50 different scents. Their wide nostrils are perfectly designed for picking up smells.

## Sight hounds

Great Danes are enormous sight hounds first bred in Germany. When standing on their back legs, they are taller than most adult humans!

The Irish wolfhound is the world's tallest dog breed—it can grow to the size of a small pony. Because of its size, it can be clumsy, but it is a gentle and sweet-natured dog.

Brrrrrr!

Greyhounds have a very short coat. This means they feel the cold, so they often need to wear a coat or a sweater in winter.

The elegant Afghan hound was first bred in the hills of Afghanistan. It has a long silky coat to keep it warm, which requires a lot of brushing to stop it from tangling.

11

# Sporting dogs

Sporting dogs are also known as hunting dogs. They were originally bred to help hunters retrieve game.

Sporting dogs are mostly kept as family pets now, since they are so loving and friendly. They still like to keep busy though, so they need lots of exercise—and love!

You throw it, I'll retrieve it!

### COCKER SPANIEL
Cocker spaniels have tons of energy and can often be found chasing squirrels up trees. They are the smallest of the sporting dogs.

Golden retrievers look very similar to Labradors, but they have a fine coat of long, golden fur.

### ENGLISH POINTER
Pointers were originally used to find small animals during a hunt. When they caught the scent of the animal being hunted, they would stand still with their noses pointing in the direction of the game.

### LABRADOR RETRIEVER
Labrador retrievers were once used by fishers in Canada to retrieve fish that had fallen from hooks back into the sea.

### LABRADOR PUPPIES
Labrador retrievers are bred in three main colours—black, chocolate, and yellow. Amazingly, a yellow Labrador retriever can have a puppy of each color all in the same litter!

They have very soft mouths, but it is probably best not to let a Labrador play with your balloon.

POP

Golden retrievers and Labrador retrievers are sweet-natured pooches and are a popular pet around the world. They love nothing more than running for a ball!

Anyone up for a game of basketball?

23

Retrievers are athletic dogs that love to run around and play ball. They are also very easy to train and often used as guide dogs, therapy dogs, and search and rescue dogs.

# Toy dogs

Toy dogs were originally bred to be family companions.

What they lack in size, they make up for in personality!

## CHIHUAHUA
Named for the Mexican state of Chihuahua, this tiny dog is one of the most popular toy breeds.

## MALTESE
These little lapdogs with fancy, long hair are an ancient breed. They were a popular pet in Roman times.

## SHIH TZU
Shih Tzus originated from Tibet. The name "Shih Tzu" means *little lion*, but they are far from fierce!

## PUG
Pugs originally came from China. They are instantly recognizable, with round, wrinkly faces and large bug-like eyes. Their fur can be silver, apricot, fawn, or black.

Hello? Peggy? Is that you?

TOYS

Pugs are very sociable dogs that love to be the center of attention at all times! They also love food, so they need plenty of exercise and outdoor playtime.

## FLAT FACES
Both pugs and Shih Tzus have been bred to have flat faces and large eyes. This has made them very popular pets, but sadly their flat muzzles mean that they can have some breathing difficulties.

The tiny Pomeranian is related to a much bigger spitz sled-dog. They are very brave and not scared of challenging bigger dogs!

Walkies!

The fluffy fur of the Pomeranian can be many different shades of white and brown and needs a lot of grooming. Some popular "fur-cuts" for Pomeranians make them look just like teddy bears!

# Terriers

Fearless and energetic, terriers were once bred to hunt vermin.

Most terriers originally came from the UK and were named after the place where they were first bred. They are mostly small dogs, trained to squeeze into animal burrows.

## BORDER TERRIER

These lively little dogs originally came from the English-Scottish borders. They have wiry coats and big personalities!

## AIREDALE TERRIER

The Airedale is the largest of all the terriers. It is very intelligent and has an excellent sense of smell.

## SKYE TERRIER

This long-haired terrier comes from Scotland. It is a very rare breed now. There are eyes and legs under that long, glossy coat!

Border terriers have lots of energy and love to chase squirrels, cats, and birds. In fact, they will chase pretty much anything that moves!

## TERRIER ATHLETICS

Terriers love to be active, and the Jack Russell is the athlete of the terrier world. It can jump up to 5 feet high!

Sadly, Staffordshire bull terriers were once trained to fight other dogs. They are actually affectionate and playful dogs with big smiles!

I'M A LOVER NOT A FIGHTER!

It's much quicker with a spade, you know.

Digging is a Jack Russell's favorite hobby, especially when it is bored. Digging a hole is more fun than being stuck indoors!

# Wolves, coyotes, and jackals

Did you know that the domestic dog is a descendent of the wolf? Let's take a walk on the wild side to look at three fascinating wild canines.

## GRAY WOLF
*Canis lupus*

The gray wolf is the largest wild canine. It lives in a variety of habitats, including forests, deserts, and grasslands, across Europe, Asia, and North America.

## COYOTE
*Canis latrans*

Native to North and Central America, coyotes are closely related to wolves. They live in family groups and will scavenge for food in urban areas.

## ETHIOPIAN WOLF
*Canis simensis*

Ethiopian wolves are one of the most endangered animals in Africa. They live in family groups and help raise one another's pups.

## BLACK-BACKED JACKAL
*Canis mesomelas*

There are only three species of jackal in the world, and this one is the smallest. It is also the most aggressive!

## MANED WOLF
*Chrysocyon brachyurus*

The maned wolf looks like a jackal or a fox with the legs of a deer—and it is not actually a wolf! It is the largest canine in South America.

## ARCTIC WOLF
*Canis lupus arctos*

This wolf is a variety of gray wolf that lives in the Arctic tundra of northern Canada and Greenland.

Gray wolves are very social creatures, living in packs of up to 30 individuals. Wolves bark, growl, and whine, but they are best known for their howling. A pack leader will howl to bring the group back together if they have been separated.

Gray wolves actually have gray and brown fur. They can also be black or even white.

Ahhh-wooooo! Sing it!

Like all canines, wolves are carnivores, which means they eat meat. They will hunt large hoofed mammals such as moose, elk, and deer, but they will also eat smaller animals, including rodents and fish.

KEEP OUT!

Wolves give birth in dens, where the pups will stay until they are big enough to travel with their pack.

# Foxes

There are over 30 different species of fox, and they are found on every continent except for Antarctica. There is one "fox" on this page that doesn't belong here. Can you spot the imposter?

## BAT-EARED FOX
*Otocyon megalotis*

The bat-eared fox lives in the grassy plains and savannah of Africa. It is named for its amazing ears, which look very similar to those of a long-eared bat.

## TIBETAN FOX
*Vulpes ferrilata*

Tibetan foxes can be found in the grasslands of Tibet, China, India, and Nepal. These square-headed foxes build their dens under boulders and rocks.

## DARWIN'S FOX
*Lycalopex fulvipes*

Darwin's fox is named after the famous naturalist Charles Darwin. Darwin discovered the fox in the 1800s on a small island off the coast of Chile. There are fewer than 1,000 of them left in the wild.

## FENNEC FOX
*Vulpes zerda*

The fennec fox is native to North Africa. It is the smallest species of fox, but it has unusually large ears.

## BENGAL FOX
*Vulpes bengalensis*

Sometimes called the Indian fox, the Bengal fox lives in the foothills of the Himalayas.

## FLYING FOX
*Yinpterochiroptera*

Don't be fooled. The flying fox is actually a type of bat and not related to the fox family at all.

## SILVER FOX
*Vulpes vulpesensis*

Silver foxes are the same species as the red fox, but they have a black or dark brown coat. In some cases the fur has white tips, which makes it appear silvery.

# ARCTIC FOX
*Vulpes lagopus*

The Arctic fox lives in the chilly Arctic tundra. This fox is small and has a big fluffy tail. Its dense white coat keeps it warm and camouflages it in the snow.

In the spring, Arctic foxes start to shed their thick white fur. It takes a few months, so they can look pretty scruffy for a while!

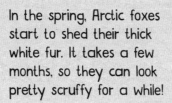

I'm feeling pretty foxy in this outfit.

By the time summer arrives, the Arctic fox has completely shed its winter coat and swapped it for a lighter brown summer coat.

The Arctic fox is an expert diver. First, it senses the movement of its prey underneath the snow. Then it dives into the snow to catch the animal it has been quietly stalking.

The urban red fox is good at diving too—mostly into trash cans. A city fox has to get its food wherever it can, so it is an expert scavenger.

# RED FOX
*Vulpes vulpes*

The red fox is the most common fox in the world. It has adapted to life in cities and rural areas, as well as in the mountains and grasslands.

# Wild dogs

There are several types of wild dog in the world. Wild dogs are undomesticated, meaning they have never lived alongside humans. There are some animals posing as dogs on this page. Can you spot the imposters?

## DHOLE
*Cuon alpinus*

There are many subspecies of this red dog living in Indonesia, China, the Himalayas, and in other parts of Asia.

## BUSH DOG
*Speothos venaticus*

The bush dog is a very rare dog living in parts of Central and South America. It has partly webbed feet, which are great for swimming.

## DINGO
*Canis familiaris dingo*

Dingoes are large wild dogs native to Australia. They often prey on animals much larger than themselves, such as the kangaroo.

## NEW GUINEA SINGING DOG
*Canis hallstromi*

The New Guinea singing dog has a distinctive, high-pitched howl that other dogs will join in with, almost like a chorus. Sadly, there are very few of them left in the wild.

## SHORT-EARED DOG
*Atelocynus microtis*

These wild dogs are found in the Amazon rainforest. They only grow to around 14 inches tall, and unusually, the females are bigger than the males.

## RACCOON DOG
*Nyctereutes procyonoides*

Much like a raccoon, the raccoon dog of East Asia looks like it is wearing a mask. It is also short and stocky. The raccoon dog is the only canine to hibernate in the winter months.

## RACCOON
*Procyon lotor*

Raccoons are NOT dogs. I just wanted to show you the similarities.

## PRAIRIE DOG
*Cynomys*

Don't let the name fool you! Prairie dogs are actually a type of rodent.

# AFRICAN PAINTED DOG
*Lycaon pictus*

The painted dog is an endangered wild dog native to Africa. Its territory can be vast, and it will cover large distances to hunt for food. Painted dogs live together in large packs made up of 7 to 15 dogs.

Painted dogs are highly social animals and will care for the pack's puppies together. If any of their packmates get sick or injured, the others will sit with them and care for them.

African painted dogs get their name from the distinct patchy brown, black, and white mottled fur that makes them look like they have been painted.

# Dogs with jobs

In the past, dogs were mainly kept to do specific jobs, such as hunting or fishing. These days most dogs live easy lives as family pets, but there are some breeds that still have important jobs to do.

## POLICE AND MILITARY DOGS

German shepherds often work with the police and the military. They even have their own police unit, called K-9. German shepherds are extremely faithful and very easy to train. They are big dogs and make excellent watch dogs.

## SEARCH AND RESCUE

As well as being great herders, collies can also be skilled search and rescue dogs. They have an excellent sense of smell and follow commands well.

MAP

It wasn't me! I did NOT steal the doggy treats, honest!

## WATER RESCUE

Newfoundlands often work with ocean rescue teams. Their webbed feet make them good swimmers, and their great strength means they are able to help pull people to safety if they get into trouble in the water.

My preferred swimming style is the dog paddle.

SEARCH AND RESCUE

# SNIFFER DOGS

Dogs have an incredible sense of smell, so they are often used as sniffer dogs. These talented canines are trained to detect the smell of illegal drugs or explosives, or to track a missing person.

Beagles can often be seen at work in airports, checking out luggage for suspicious smells.

# ASSISTANCE DOGS

Labradors are often used as assistance (or guide) dogs. This gentle breed can be trained to help people who are visually impaired or those who are deaf or hard of hearing.

Guide dogs are trained to know when it's safe to cross a road. They can also remember the regular routes of their visually impaired human companion.

GUIDE DOG

# THERAPY DOGS

Many breeds of dog, such as poodles, retrievers, and pugs, can be trained to provide emotional support. Therapy dogs are often taken to visit patients in a hospital. Petting a dog can make people feel happy!

# Communication

Dogs communicate in many different ways—it's not all about yipping and woofing. Dogs use their whole bodies to communicate with us and with each other.

## WAGGING TAIL

A tail wagging in a circular motion lets us know that the dog is happy. Some dogs wiggle their entire bottoms when they wag their tails!

## TUCKED TAIL

Another sign that a dog is feeling scared or stressed is when it curls its tail down between its legs.

## TEETH

Dogs will growl and bare their teeth when they feel threatened by another dog or a human.

## EARS

A dog will flatten its ears to the back of its head when it feels scared.

## SNIFFING

All dogs love to sniff. It's their way to greet another dog. By sniffing, they can find out if the other dog is male or female, healthy and happy.

They sniff each other's noses . . .

. . . and each other's butts. Ewww!

26

## PLAYFUL

You can tell when dogs are in a playful mood. They will roll over onto their backs or lower their front paws, sticking their bottoms up in the air. It means "I am ready to play!"

## DOG TRAINING

Domestic dogs can be trained to respond to commands such as sit, heel, lie down, and "paw." Dogs will often offer their paw as a sign of affection and to gain their owner's attention.

Give me your paw!

Nope!

## HOWLING

Some dogs will howl when their owners leave them home alone. They love to be with their people so much.

Aw-rooo!

Woof woof!

MAIL

## BARKING

It can be annoying, but many dogs will bark when somebody knocks at the door. It is their way of announcing "this is MY house!"

## MARKING TERRITORY

Dogs and other canines mark their territory with their urine. It is a message to other dogs that they have been there.

Sniff sniff!

# Agility training

Pet dogs need to be exercised daily. Most are full of energy, and if they don't run off some steam they can get bored and destructive. Dog agility classes can be a great way to exercise both the body and the mind of a dog.

Agility training is a competitive sport where dogs can compete to win trophies.

Dogs can be trained to weave quickly through poles . . .

People also take their dogs to agility courses just for fun and exercise. They are just like doggy playgrounds!

Some canines, however, prefer to run free!

. . . and jump through rings
and run through tunnels.

They can even be trained to run
along a seesaw!

Some canines are easier
to train for agility than
others. Border collies,
Labradors, and Jack
Russells are good, but
foxes are not so willing
to learn!

I am going for gold!

Greyhounds, African painted dogs,
and gray wolves are great runners.
Wild dogs can sprint in short bursts
to catch prey and will cover great
distances when hunting.

# Map of wild canines

These are the places you're most likely to see the wild canines in this book. Most breeds of pet dog can be found all over the world, but wild canines are less widespread.

## NORTH AMERICA
The gray wolf is the largest of all the wild canines found in America. Though smaller than the wolf, the coyote is a hugely successful dog that has spread to every US state apart from Hawaii.

## EUROPE
There are three types of wild canine in Europe: the red fox, the Arctic fox, and the gray wolf. Once heavily hunted, the gray wolf is gradually being reintroduced to many European countries.

## SOUTH AMERICA
South America is home to wild dogs, foxes, and wolves. The magnificent maned wolf can be found in grasslands and forests all across the continent.

## AFRICA
Africa is home to a wide variety of wild canine, including the bat-eared fox and the Ethiopian wolf. Wild dogs, such as the African painted dog, are also native to Africa. Sadly, they are endangered.

## PET DOGS
The domesticated dog is related to the wolf, which was first kept as a companion by humans some 12,000 years ago. Humans love dogs because they make such loyal companions.

## ASIA

Asia is home to many wild dogs, one of which is the dhole. It lives in various habitats in Central, South, and Southeast Asia. The dhole is extremely endangered, mostly due to hunting and disease. Asia also has many species of fox, including the Tibetan, Bengal, and red fox.

## AUSTRALASIA

Australia has just one wild canine: the dingo. It is a descendent of the New Guinea singing dog of Papua New Guinea. The dingo is a skilled hunter. It will eat anything, from large mammals through to birds and reptiles.

# Mixed breeds

A mixed-breed dog (or mongrel) is the result of different breeds of dogs having puppies together. These pooches are usually sweet-natured and friendly, and they make great family pets.

Hi there! My name is Peggy.

Cockapoo

## NEW BREEDS

Sometimes, when a dog is the result of two recognized breeds of dog, it can become a breed all of its own! Can you guess the mix of these three dogs?

Chug

Borgi

I'm Bob the dog!

## MONGRELS

A mongrel can have many different breeds in its family line. They can have the coat of one type of dog, the ears of another, and the legs of an altogether different breed of dog!

Hi. My name is Sara. I am a very good dog!

## RESCUE DOGS

Rescue shelters give food, love, and a warm bed to dogs that do not have a home. It is a good thing to adopt a dog from a shelter, but there are lots of things to consider before getting a pet. Somebody will need to walk the dog every day, and you need patience to train a dog and take care of it.